GERANIUMS

Margaret Stone

HPS
HARDY PLANT SOCIETY
Gardening with hardy perennials

Hardy geraniums have been grown in British gardens for many years. This print is of *G. sylvaticum* 'Angulatum', which was first described as *G. angulatum* and then *G. sylvaticum var. angulatum*; the illustration is from William Curtis, The *Botanical Magazine or Flower Garden Displayed*, volume V, plate 203 (London: Curtis, 1792). Image courtesy Missouri Botanical Garden www.botanicus.org

This series of booklets, produced and published by the Hardy Plant Society, covers some of the most popular garden genera and some of the more unusual ones. Written by specialists in their field, each booklet contains cultivation and propagation advice with a descriptive list of some good garden-worthy varieties. They may be ordered by contacting the HPS Administrator; details can be found at www.hardy-plant.org.uk

Front cover: *Geranium pratense* 'Mrs Kendall Clark'
Author: Joy Jones, revised by Margaret Stone
Editor: Irene Tibbenham
Printed by

Design, Print & Marketing Services
Web: www.rprint.co.uk

Front cover design & typesetting by Goyle Weir, goyle@mac.com
©Hardy Plant Society May 2015
ISBN: 978-0-901687-29-6

Gardening with hardy perennials

Hardy Plant Society

Formed in 1957 by a group of eminent gardeners and nurserymen, this international Society has a large UK and overseas membership. It provides members with information about familiar and less-well-known perennials, and their cultivation. Through conservation and publicity, the Society works towards ensuring that all garden-worthy perennial plants remain in cultivation and have the widest possible distribution.

The Hardy Plant Society welcomes new members to join; please telephone the administrator on 01386 710 317 for details; or complete an application form from our website, www.hardy-plant.org.uk

The charitable objectives of the Society are:

a) to advance the culture, study and improvement of hardy herbaceous plants,
b) to preserve the older, rarer and lesser known hardy plants, cultivars and varieties from being forgotten and lost to cultivation,
c) to advance the knowledge of and foster public interest in hardy plants by the publication of information, by exhibitions or displays, by stimulating research and experiment and by awarding bursaries open to public competition,
d) to provide expositions of hardy plants at horticultural gardens and/or gardens open to the public, and to provide facilities for giving advice on the culture of hardy plants,
e) to organise visits to places of interest in connection with the study of hardy plants and to co-operate with other bodies having similar or sympathetic aims,
f) to do such acts as shall further the active and corporate life of the Society and which may lawfully be done by a public body established only for purposes recognised by the laws of the United Kingdom as charitable.

Some of these objects are achieved through the publication of booklets such as this one on Geraniums.

www.hardy-plant.org.uk

Registered Charity No 208080

CONTENTS

Acknowledgements

Joy Jones

The introduction on the following page accompanied previous editions of this book and was written by Joy Jones, who died in June 2013. She was Chairman and then Honorary President and Life President of the Hardy Geranium Group. The present membership dedicates this new edition to her.

Margaret Stone

Margaret gardens in Callow End, Worcestershire, where she holds Plant Heritage National Plant Collections® of *Geranium* x *cantabrigiense*, *macrorrhizum* and *sanguineum*. She is currently chairman of the HPS Geranium Group.

David Victor

Access to the Register of Geranium Cultivar names was provided by David X Victor, former Chairman and now Honorary President of the HPS Hardy Geranium Group. David, who lives in Somerset, is interested in all the Geraniaceae and holds a Plant Heritage National Plant Collection® of *Pelargonium* xerophytic clade.

Photograph Contributors

Adrian James, Alan Whitehead, Ann Hooper, Blooms of Bressingham®, Carrie Thomas, David Victor, Don Witton, Eleanor Fisher, Ilja Smit-Kroon, Irene Tibbenham, Jennifer Harmer, John McCormack, Ken Mines – Picket Lane Nursery, Margaret Stone, Ruth Jowett, Tim Fuller – The Plantsman's Preference, Trevor Hards, Trevor Walton, Tricia Fraser

Photographic credits — see page 60

Thanks go to Sandra Hartley, Tim Fuller and members of the Hardy Geranium Group for assistance with text proofing.

Introduction
Joy Jones

To many people the name 'geranium' still relates to the exotic, tender bedding plants, so popular in the Victorian era, which are now botanically *Pelargonium*. Old habits die hard and so there is a lot of confusion when 'hardy geraniums' are mentioned. It is with these, the true *Geranium* or cranesbill (referring to the beak-like seed structure), that we are concerned in this booklet. To confuse matters further, there are a few geraniums that are not entirely hardy in the British Isles. Nevertheless, the majority are able to withstand the coldest winters, easy to grow, practically disease free, usually ignored by pests, tolerant of different soil conditions and able to thrive in sun or half shade (some deep shade).

Newcomers to gardening are well advised to start with some of the 'easy' species, with the hope they will be further encouraged to collect more varieties. My first introduction to gardening was on heavy blue clay (adjoining the local brick fields). Everything I planted rotted or was devoured by slugs or smothered by pernicious weeds – until someone gave me *Geranium* × *magnificum*, which did so well I was soon on the road to geranium addiction.

Some species have been grown in our gardens for over four hundred years. Today the choice is very much wider and discerning gardeners recognise a geranium exists for every situation. Ideal for informal cottage gardens, they are equally at home in more formal plantings. Their leaves vary in shape, size and texture. Indeed some are even pleasantly aromatic. Is it the simplicity of the flowers that makes cranesbills appealing or perhaps their ability to mingle successfully with other plants!

You may ask do they have any disadvantages! Perhaps one is the profusion with which some species disperse their seedlings. This can be a problem, especially in small gardens. Nevertheless, once you have learned to recognise the seedlings, unwanted ones are easily removed when small. Should you have ground to spare, these can be grown on, just in case you have an exciting new hybrid. Another complaint is that some become untidy after the main flush of flowers, particularly *G. endressii* and *G.* × *oxonianum* and their forms. Shearing foliage to the ground is the answer. This should result in a fresh crop of foliage and flowers, but do water in dry weather after this treatment.

Getting to know geraniums is an enjoyable pastime; many can be seen by visiting specialist nurseries and botanic gardens. Literature on geraniums is scarce. The late Margery Fish stimulated interest with her books, such as *Ground Cover Plants, Gardening in the Shade* and *Cottage Garden Flowers. Hardy Geraniums* by Dr Peter Yeo of Cambridge University was first published in 1985, after many years of research into the genus. This authoritative work has clarified the confusion surrounding the previous naming of many species. It has also inspired gardeners to seek rarer varieties. Further knowledge can be gained by joining specialist societies, such as The Hardy Plant Society, which runs a Hardy Geranium Group.

Geraniums as Garden Plants

Margaret Stone

"When in doubt, plant a geranium." Margery Fish

Hardy geraniums constitute a group of plants which offer solutions to many gardening problems. Examples can be found in flower from spring to autumn and some have useful over-wintering leaves. Their heights vary from a few centimetres to over a metre and the flower colours range from blue, through purple and magenta, to pink and white. Some do best in sunny well-drained positions, whilst others prefer shade or moist soil but the majority are not fussy. Individual plants can grow happily for thirty years or more so they are ideal for those seeking a low-maintenance garden; however, their variety offers plenty to the enthusiast and they can become addictive!

Most species have flowering stems which die back after flowering, leaving a clump of foliage for the remainder of the season. Clumps can be compact e.g. *G. renardii* or spreading, such as *G. macrorrhizum*, which is frequently used as ground cover. Some die down after flowering: *G. libani* is dormant from early summer until September so can tolerate other plants spreading across it then. Length of flowering is variable: *G.* × *magnificum* is a mass of flowers for a few weeks, 'Azure Rush' continues for five months.

This booklet aims to provide the gardener with information to choose an appropriate geranium for a given situation. It may be assumed that all varieties can be planted in ordinary soil in an open or partially shaded position, unless otherwise described.

Some geraniums for shade

(*indicates suitable for dry shade): *G. gracile, G. kishtvariense, G. macrorrhizum** (but not 'Variegatum'), *G. nodosum*, G.* × *oxonianum* e.g. 'Claridge Druce'*, *G. phaeum*, G. pyrenaicum*, G. shikokianum*

Geraniums for sunny, well-drained sites

G. caffrum, G. 'Carol', *G. cinereum, G. dalmaticum, G. farreri, G. harveyi, G. lindavicum,* 'Little Gem', 'Orkney Pink', *G. riversleaianum, G. sanguineum, G. sessiliflorum*

For damper sites

G. maculatum, G. richardsonii, G. palustre, G. soboliferum

It is good practice to add garden compost to the planting hole but further feeding is unnecessary. Staking is optional. Some borders are close packed so that plants support each other; in others geraniums are allowed to flop into wide clumps. Old clumps of *G. himalayense* do tend to develop a doughnut shape: just when a clump is looking magnificent, heavy rain will knock it down so that the flowers fall into a circle with an empty centre. Early staking can avoid this but it is better to divide plants every three to five years.

Geranium 'Brookside'

Foliage

The basic leaf shape has five points. Sometimes the sections have shallow notches and indentations but more often they are divided and subdivided into all sorts of pleasingly different patterns. Sometimes the size and shape of the main basal leaves differ from the leaves borne on the flowering stems. In some of the smaller-growing varieties the leaves give a general impression of being more circular than pointed but within that shape the divisions tend to be more intricate and lacy.

Good variegation is found in the leaves of *G. macrorrhizum* 'Variegatum', *G. orientalitibeticum* (which spreads vigorously), *G. phaeum* 'Margaret Wilson' and *G. phaeum* 'Variegatum'. Some young leaves start with a golden flush which fades as the leaf matures: *G.* 'Ann Folkard', *G.* 'Blue Sunrise', *G.* × *oxonianum* 'Spring Fling'. The leaves of *G.* × *oxonianum* typically have five brown spots between the lobes but these sometimes increase to larger blotches e.g. in 'Walter's Gift', which is striking in spring. *G. phaeum* shows a similar effect: 'Calligrapher' and 'Samobor' have good dark markings all season. *G. pratense* Midnight Reiter strain has all-over dark foliage; 'Pink Spice' is attractively pewter in colour and *G. sessiliflorum* subsp. *novae-zelandiae* 'Nigricans' is a small plant with dark-brown leaves.

Many geraniums colour well in autumn, particularly *G. sanguineum* and *G. macrorrhizum*. In *G. macrorrhizum* the older leaves turn yellow and red before dying, leaving young evergreen foliage (not 'Variegatum'). Other winter-greens are

G. maculatum 'Elizabeth Ann '

G. 'Salome'

G. phaeum 'Samobor'

G. nodosum

G. phaeum 'Conny Broe'

G. phaeum 'Lisa'

G. 'Tanya Rendall'

G. 'Sanne'

G. libani and the finely cut *G. malviflorum*, both of which are summer dormant. *G. palmatum* is a good evergreen plant given the necessary shelter but *G. maderense* is even better though more tender.

If ground-covering foliage is required, *G. × cantabrigiense*, *G. macrorrhizum*, *G. × oxonianum* and *G. phaeum* can be recommended. These last two should have the flowering stems removed in July. Some people shear the whole plant back, leaving it bare, but it is better to leave the foliage and remove the flowering stems only. In a sunny, well-drained, site *G.* 'Sanne' makes a dense carpet about 1m diameter each summer but it dies back in late autumn, leaving a permanent mound of dark foliage about 30 cm across. *G. schlechteri* behaves in a similar way but is taller (~50 cm) and has silvery-green leaves.

Several geraniums have leaves with good texture but the best is *G. renardii*, velvety to the touch. *G. macrorrhizum* has highly aromatic foliage.

G. phaeum 'Golden Samobor'

Propagation

For established stocks of geraniums, division is the easiest method of increasing the number of plants. A whole clump of a variety such as G. × oxonianum can be lifted in early spring, pulled apart and replanted; it will need watering until established. Most of the vigorous, clump-forming species can be divided every third year. It is also possible to remove rooted side-shoots from spreading species such as G. clarkei, G. dalmaticum and G. macrorrhizum at any time of year. Tuberous species (e.g. G. malviflorum, G. orientalitibeticum) can have small tubers removed from the main clump, while dormant. G. procurrens has long trailing stems which root at the nodes and can be potted up like strawberry runners. (The rooting habit makes this geranium unsuitable for situations where a small, 'tidy' plant is required.) Intriguingly, hybrids bred from G. procurrens do not have this rooting habit making them excellent garden plants, e.g. 'Ann Folkard', 'Anne Thomson', 'Salome'. They can be propagated by basal cuttings taken in spring, before the long stems develop. G. wallichianum cultivars are treated similarly, e.g. 'Azure Rush', HAVANA BLUES,[PBR] 'Sweet Heidy'. Some geraniums form a rosette around a single growing point e.g. G. cinereum. These can provide cuttings at any time of year but are difficult to root.

Geranium species will reproduce reliably from seed; cultivars do not usually come true but can give interesting results. Gritty, loam-based seed compost should be used and not multi-purpose compost. Seed-sown pots can be left outside but do not need frost to break dormancy and will germinate in a frost-free or warm location.

Collecting seed sometimes confuses people and gardeners are known to have harvested empty seed cases thinking they were seed. The fruit of geraniums is long and narrow, like a bird's beak, and their name comes from the Greek word geranos, a crane; hence, they are known as 'cranesbills'. As the seeds ripen, the 'beak' turns dark brown or black. At this point the fruits can be picked, even though the seed cases may still be green. They will continue to ripen if kept in a paper bag or envelope. The bag must be closed because ripe fruits explode. This is their natural method of dispersal, the energetic ejection ensuring that seed falls away from the parent plant. In some species a naked column is left behind but in most species the seed cases remain attached to the column. If the seed cases are already black, cup the fruit in your hand before picking because they often explode as they are picked. It is sensible to feel seed cases when picking to ensure they contain a plump, hard, viable seed. Sterile hybrids often produce seed cases but fail to develop seed.

Pests and Diseases

In the ground geraniums are troubled by few pests although the leaves can be eaten by molluscs and winter caterpillars. Pot-grown specimens are frequently attacked by vine weevils, particularly if grown in multi-purpose compost. It is better to use gritty, loam-based compost. If plants are to be overwintered, it is worth repotting them in autumn or early spring and checking for grubs.

In most conditions geraniums are healthy plants which do not suffer greatly from disease. Rust can occur and G. pratense is susceptible to mildew. Cut mildewed foliage to the ground and keep well watered. The most potentially serious problem is summer root-rot, in which the ground becomes waterlogged turning the stems black; death follows quickly. Though uncommon, it attacks *G. cinereum* and *G. macrorrhizum*.

Joy Jones, *revised by* Margaret Stone

The following list includes most geraniums known to be in cultivation. Some may be difficult to track down but, fortunately, there exist some excellent nurseries specializing in hardy geraniums. Consider searching through seed lists to track down species geraniums.

Hybrids sometimes show the name of the breeder. Notable geranium breeders include **Alan Bremner**, from Orkney, who has carried out a major long-term programme. **Alan Bloom** worked on alpine species and Blooms of Bressingham, Norfolk, have since introduced other plants. **Robin Moss** is from Hexham, Northumberland, and **Cyril Foster** also lives in Northumberland. **Jenny Spiller** runs Elworthy Cottage Plants, Somerset, and **Tim Fuller,** The Plantsman's Preference in Norfolk, which he started with his mother, the late **Jenny Fuller**. **John Tuite** is from Westacre Gardens, Norfolk. **Coen Jansen, Hans Kramer** and **Marco van Noort** are Dutch nurserymen; **Ivan Louette** works in Belgium and **Hans Simon** in Germany.

The name of the plant is followed by:

- Other names under which it may be found
- ^{PBR} Plant Breeders' Rights which give exclusive propagation control to the plant's originator
- ^{RHS} 🏆 Award of Garden Merit; this geranium has been awarded the Royal Horticultural Society's Award of Garden Merit (AGM) meaning it performs well and will thrive in most garden conditions

- Its parentage if a hybrid; places of origin; breeder
- ‡ Approximate height (which will vary according to soil and situation)
- Flowering time (again variable)
- Flower size, referring to the approximate diameter

G. 'Alan Mayes'

G. 'Alan Mayes' (× *G. platypetalum*?) ‡40—55cm May—Jul. Clump-forming with hairy leaves. Plentiful deep-blue 4cm flowers with darker-blue veins. Sun; drought tolerant.

G. 'Alan's Blue' (*G.* 'Kashmir White' × *G. saxatilis* × *G. pratense var. stewartianum*) (Bremner) ‡50—70cm Jun—Jul. Vigorous plant; light-blue, veined flowers with a white eye.

G. albanum SE Caucasus and adjacent parts of Iran ‡30—45cm Jun—Jul. Summer dormant, forms substantial clumps of winter leaves. Flowers 2cm, pink with magenta veins, on long, thin, trailing stems. Rather untidy in habit but useful where it has space to weave through neighbouring branches.

G. albiflorum N & C Asia, NE European Russia ‡30cm May onwards. Low growing with deeply divided leaves; stems, leaf margins and sepals purplish-brown. Flowers, small, funnel shaped, white or palest lilac, violet-veined, produced spasmodically over a long period. Prefers light shade.

G. anemonifolium see G. palmatum

G. 'Ann Folkard' ᴿᴴˢ🏆 *(G. procurrens × G. psilostemon)* ‡40cm An almost sterile hybrid raised by Oliver Folkard in 1973. This outstanding plant produces a mass of golden-tinted foliage in spring from a comparatively small crown, later turning green. Very long, thin non-rooting stems cover a wide area, scrambling through other plants. Flowers approximately 4cm, magenta with black centre and veins. Flowering non-stop from July to autumn.

G. 'Ann Folkard'

G. 'Anne Thomson' ᴿᴴˢ🏆 *(G. procurrens × G. psilostemon)* (Bremner) ‡50 × 90cm Jun—Oct, non-stop. From the same parentage as G. 'Ann Folkard', with a similar flower, but is a more upright, compact plant with copious flowers massed above the foliage. Border in sun.

G. × *antipodeum* *(G. traversii × G. sessiliflorum)* ‡25cm June onwards. **'Black Ice'** (Bremner) forms large neat mounds of dark bronze foliage from which radiate long stems carrying small white, occasionally blush-pink, flowers. **'Buckland Beauty'** has bronze-green trailing foliage ‡15—20cm and 1.5cm magenta-pink flowers. **'Chocolate Candy'**'ᴾᴮᴿ (Jansen) was a seedling from 'Stanhoe' found in 1992; dark leaves, pale pink flowers. It is not fully hardy, needing sharp drainage in full sun and winter protection in cold damp areas. **'Pink Spice'**'ᴾᴮᴿ has a spreading habit with annual flower stems; pink flowers. The result of seed-selection in New Zealand. **'Purple Passion'**'ᴾᴮᴿ has purple flowers and foliage and **'Rothbury Red'** (Foster) has white flowers, flushed pink with a darker eye, and reddish foliage. **'Sea Spray'** (Bremner) has very pale pink flowers with olive foliage spreading to more than 1m. **'Stanhoe'** is a seedling from a garden in Stanhoe, Norfolk, 1979; compact green plant with pale-pink flowers.

G. 'Apple Blossom' see G. × lindavicum

G. 'Anne Thomson'

G. aristatum S Europe ‡45cm Jun—Aug. A distinctive hairy plant forming hummocks of greyish-green leaves. Flowers 2.5cm nodding, petals strongly reflexed, white or pale-lilac, attractively veined with violet. Reliable and worthy of a place in the border.

G. a. subsp. *asphodeloides*

G. asphodeloides S Europe ‡30cm Apr—Jul. Evergreen rounded leaves for borders, banks and walls. *G. a.* **subsp.** *asphodeloides* is the most common subspecies. Numerous starry flowers, 2.5cm, pale to deep mauvish-pink, strongly veined with reddish-purple. **'Prince Regent'** has pale-lilac flowers and **'Starlight'** is white. *G. a.* subsp. *crenophilum* has rose-pink flowers with broad petals. *G. a.* **subsp.** *sintenisii*, very free-flowering plant with pale-pink or purple flowers.

G. 'Azure Rush'′PBR (× *G. wallichianum*) ‡40cm June onwards. Bred from Rozanne but more compact. 5cm light violet-blue flowers with a white centre.

G. 'Azzurro'′PBR (× *G. wallichianum*) (van Noort) ‡30cm July onwards. Light-blue 4cm flowers, violet veins, white centre. Not totally hardy.

G. 'Bertie Crûg' (*G. antipodeum* × *G. papuanum*) ‡5cm spreading. A seedling found in the nursery at Crûg Farm plants and named after the nursery terrier! This diminutive creeper develops mats of shiny bronze leaves and small purplish-pink flowers over a long period. Borderline hardy; it needs good drainage in a rock garden or scree.

G. biuncinatum (annual), Africa, Arabia ‡20cm. Flowers deep-pink, 2cm, with a dark centre.

G. 'Blue Blood' (*G. gymnocaulon* × *G. ibericum* subsp. *jubatum*) ‡50cm Jun—Jul. 5cm violet-blue flowers.

G. 'Blue Cloud' ᴿᴴˢ ♈ (possibly from 'Nimbus') ‡90cm May—Aug. Light mauve-blue, 4cm, 'gappy' flowers.

G. **'Blue Cloud'**

G. 'Blogold'′PBR Blue Sunrise ᴿᴴˢ ♈ (*G. wallichianum* 'Buxton's Variety' × *G.* 'Ann Folkard') (Kramer) ‡30cm. This has inherited the best of both parents: golden spring foliage of 'Ann Folkard' (which lasts longer) and (larger) deep-blue flowers of 'Buxton's Variety' all summer.

G. 'Blushing Turtle'[PBR] *(G. sanguineum ×
G. × oxonianum* or *G. asphodeloides)* ‡40—
60cm June onwards. 2.5cm flowers, soft
pink with deeper-pink-veins.

G. 'Blushing Turtle'[PBR]

G. 'Bob's Blunder' (unknown parentage)
‡20cm Jun—Oct. A perennial cushion
of light-brown leaves from which
progressively come elongating annual
flowering stems. Pale-pink 2cm flowers.

G. bohemicum (annual/biennial) E & C
Europe ‡30—50cm, lavender-blue 2cm
flowers.

G. 'Brookside' [RHS] ♛ *(G. pratense × G. clarkei*
'Kashmir Purple') (Cambridge Botanic
Garden) ‡60cm Jun—Aug. Clumps of
finely cut foliage on reddish stems. 4cm
flowers are bowl shaped (petals overlap),
deep blue, with a white eye.

G. brutium (annual) Italy, Sicily, Balkan
Peninsula, Turkey ‡30cm. A mound of light-
green, rounded leaves and a profusion of
small bright-bluish-pink flowers enhanced
by bluish-black anthers. It self-seeds
moderately, especially in gravel and
between cracks in paving.

G. 'Buxton's Blue' see *G. wallichianum*
'Buxton's Variety'

G. caeruleatum Balkan mountains,
Carpathians ‡25cm May—Jun. Neat plant
with deeply divided leaves. Numerous
light-blue 1.5cm flowers.

G. caffrum S Africa ‡60cm Jun—Jul. Grows
from thick taproot; slender stems, woody
at the base. Leaves very deeply cut with
narrow lobes and sharply toothed. Flowers
small but prolific, usually white, sometimes
pink. Reasonably hardy in light soil; self-
sows quite freely.

G. canariense see *G. reuteri*

G. × cantabrigiense *(G. dalmaticum × G.
macrorrhizum)* ‡30cm late May to early
July. Compact mats of glossy, aromatic,
evergreen foliage, spreading steadily
but not rampantly; good autumn colour.
Flowers 2.5cm, light-pink, abundantly
produced. Leaves and flowers midway
between parents. **'Harz'** and **'St Ola'** are
white while **'Biokovo'** is white with pink
veins, less dense growth. **'Berggarten'**,
'Cambridge' and **'Karmina'** are deep
pink, **'Abpp'** Crystal Rose[PBR] shocking
pink, **'Hanne'** pink with a white edge and
'Westray'[PBR] bright-pink.

G. St Ola'   **G. 'Berggarten'**

G. cataractarum S Spain, Morocco ‡30cm
June onwards. Aromatic, deeply divided,

ferny, evergreen leaves. Flowers 2cm, funnel shaped, bright pink with orange-red anthers. Rock garden or trough in half shade. Moderately hardy, though not very long lived.

G. 'Catherine Deneuve'[PBR]

G. 'Catherine Deneuve'[PBR] ↕50—80cm May—Sep. A chance seedling found near *G. psilostemon* and *G. procurrens* but *G.* × *oxonianum* f. *thurstonianum* seems to be a more likely parent than *G. procurrens*. The 4cm flowers have narrow, widely separated petals; they are deep magenta-pink with dark veins and centre.

G. 'Chantilly' (*G. gracile* × *G. renardii*) (Bremner) ↕45cm May—Aug. Clouds of lavender-pink flowers with separated notched petals; leaves similar to *G. renardii* but larger. An upright plant which seems to prefer some shade that is not too dry.

G. cinereum Group C Pyrenees ↕15cm mid-May—Jul. Neat rosettes of small, rounded, divided leaves of greyish green. Flowers 4cm on lax stems, white or pink, finely pencilled with darker veins. Rock garden, scree or trough; gritty soil in sun. **'Album'** is a pure white form; **'Alice'**[PBR] is pale lilac-pink. **'Ballerina'** ⚘ (Bloom) flowers 3cm purple-pink, with dark veins and a dark blotch at the base; attractive

G. cinereum 'Album'

G. cinereum 'Alice'[PBR]

G. cinereum 'Laurence Flatman'

G. cinereum 'Memories'

G. cinereum 'Purple Pillow'

G. cinereum ROTHBURY GEM^PBR

G. cinereum 'Sateene'^PBR

and reliable. **'Carol'** bright-cerise flowers, veined and with a dark eye; free flowering. **'Laurence Flatman'** (Bloom) is similar to 'Ballerina' but with alternating pale and dark patches on the petals; **'Memories'**^PBR has red-purple flowers and **'Purple Pillow'** is purple. **'Gerfos'**^PBR ROTHBURY GEM^PBR ♈ (Foster) ‡10cm with 3cm pale-purple flowers with a red eye. **'Sateene'**^PBR is purple pink and **'Thumbling Hearts'** has pink flowers with black centres.

G. clarkei Kashmir ‡45cm June onwards. Finely cut leaves, spreading by underground rhizomes. Purple flowers, 4cm, facing upwards. **'Kashmir Pink'** is light pink, **'Kashmir Purple'** deep violet-purple, red veins. **'Kashmir White'** is white with delicate lilac-pink veins, giving a mauvish-grey flush. **'Mount Stewart'** is white with deep lilac-pink veins.

G. clarkei 'Mount Stewart'

G. collinum SE Europe, C & E Turkey, W & C Asia ‡45—60cm Jun—Sep. Bushy clumps of finely cut grey-green leaves. Flowers 3cm, saucer shaped, usually mid-pink but can be lighter or darker. Useful in the border for its long flowering period and resistance to drought conditions, properties which have led to its use in breeding.

G. `Coombland White' (*G. lambertii* × *G. traversii*) ‡30cm, spreading. Raised by the late Rosemary Lee of Coombland Nursery.

G. `Coombland White'

Makes large hummocks of rounded mottled leaves with long trailing stems. The flowers are comparable to those of *G. lambertii* '**Swansdown**', white with lilac veins converging to a dark-violet centre. Grow in full sun and well-drained soil and allow plenty of space. May need winter protection in cold, wet soil.

G. 'Criss Canning' (*G. pratense* × *G. himalayense*) ‡30cm June onwards. Blue with dark veins and white eye, 4cm, sun.

G. 'Criss Canning'

G. 'Cyril's Fancy' (*G. sylvaticum* × *G. albiflorum*) (Foster) ‡30 × 90cm, Jul—Oct. A robust plant resembling *G. sylvaticum* with large leaves and many large, pale lilac flowers with widely spaced petals.

G. 'Cyril's Fancy'

G. dahuricum NE Asia, W China ‡45cm Jun—Aug. A sprawler with thin lax stems, small finely cut leaves with narrow, rather widely spaced lobes. New leaves emerging in spring are delicate pink and cream. Flowers 3cm, saucer shaped, pale pink with dark-red veins, sun.

G. dalmaticum ℞ SW Europe, Albania ‡10—15cm Jun—Jul. Slowly spreading, neat hummocks of evergreen, aromatic, shiny leaves; good autumn tints. Flowers 2cm, pale pink, held well above the foliage. Responds to frequent division; sun. '**Album**' is white; '**Bressingham Pink**' is deeper pink than the type and '**Bridal**

G. *dalmaticum*'Album'

G. 'Devon Pride'

G. `Dilys' ^{RHS} 🏆 (*G. sanguineum* × *G. procurrens*) (Bremner) ‡25cm Jul—Sep. Named after Dilys Davies, a former HPS chairman. The foliage, very similar to *G. sanguineum*, is produced on long trailing stems (non-rooting) with 3cm reddish-purple, dark-eyed flowers.

Bouquet' opens pale pink fading to almost white.

G. 'Danny Boy' ^{RHS} 🏆 (*G. wlassovianum* × *G. palustre*?) ‡50cm spreading to 1.5m Jun-Jul. Magenta flowers, 3.5cm.

G. 'Deux Fleurs' (*G. sanguineum* × *G.* × *oxonianum*?) (Louette) ‡30—40cm Jun—Sep. A vigorous plant with two 5cm reddish-pink flowers on most stems.

G. 'Devon Pride' (*G.* × *oxonianum*? × *G. psilostemon*?) ‡60cm June onwards. Pale green foliage; plentiful 3cm light magenta flowers with black centres. Similar to PATRICIA but with smaller flowers and lower growing; sun.

G. `Dilys'

G. 'Distant Hills (*G. pratense* × *G. collinium*) ‡40cm Jun—Aug. Pale purple-blue 3cm flowers.

G. 'Diva' (*G. sanguineum* × *G. swatense*) ↕25—40cm Jun—Sep. The new foliage is golden. Purple-red 3cm flowers.

G. donianum Himalayas, SW China, Tibet ↕15—45cm Deeply divided, marbled leaves from thick rootstock. Flowers funnel-shaped, upwardly inclined, reddish purple. Not very long lived but easily raised from seed.

G. 'Bremdra'[PBR] **DRAGON HEART** (*G. psilostemon* × *G. procurrens*) (Bremner) ↕60cm June onwards. 5cm magenta flowers with a black centre.

G. 'Castle Drogo'

G. 'Bremdream'[PBR] **DREAMLAND** (*G. traversii* × *G. oxonianum*) (Bremner) ↕20cm grey-green foliage; 3cm light-pink flowers all summer.

G. 'Dusky Crûg' (*G. antipodeum* × *G. oxonianum*) ↕20cm Jun—Oct. Pale pink, 2cm; deep-brown foliage. Sun; good drainage.

G. 'Dusky Rose' (*G. sessiliflorum* 'Nigricans' hybrid) ↕20cm Jun—Oct. Dark foliage; pale-pink 2cm flowers. Sun; well drained.

G. 'Elke' see *G. sanguineum*

G. `Elworthy Dusky' (Spiller) ↕30cm May—Jul. Probably a seedling from *G.* 'Brookside'; the substantial clumps bear clouds of dusky-pink flowers. Sun.

G. 'Elworthy Eyecatcher' (*G. endressii*? × *G. wallichianum*) (Spiller) ↕45cm June onwards. Deep-pink 3cm flowers.

G. 'Elworthy Tiger' (*G. himalayense* × ?) (Spiller) ↕15cm Jun—Jul. 3cm blue flowers with darker veins.

G. endressii [RHS]♕ S Europe, W Asia ↕45cm Jun—Sep. Light-green, almost evergreen, divided and pointed leaves providing dense colonising ground cover. Flowers 3cm, funnel shaped, bright chalky-pink with notched petals. **'Castle Drogo'** [RHS]♕ 40cm spreading to 1m+. Bright pink flowers fade with age.

G. erianthum E Siberia, Japan, Alaska, Canada (N. BC) ↕45—60cm May—Jun and later. Resembles *G. platyanthum* but leaves more deeply divided. Good autumn colour. Flowers 4cm, flattish, varying from pale to rich violet-blue and darkly veined. **'Calm Sea'** is taller than the type, with soft grey-blue flowers; **'Neptune'** has larger,

G. 'Neptune'

deeper blue flowers. **'Pale Blue Yonder'** (Moss) is pale blue without veins, **'Undine'** is shorter, pure white.

G. eriostemon see *G. platyanthum*

G. 'Eureka Blue' ‡60cm Jun—Sep. Vigorous sport from 'Orion'. Lavender-blue flowers 4cm+.

G. farreri W China ‡10—15cm May—Jun. Introduced by Farrer in 1917. Small, rounded, divided leaves, reddish margins and stems. Flowers 3cm, soft pink with conspicuous bluish-black anthers. Well-drained, gritty soil in full sun.

G. fremontii W N America ‡30—45cm Jun—Sep. A distinctive sticky, hairy geranium with numerous deeply divided leaves, coarsely lobed and toothed. Flowering stems much branched and leafy. Flowers 4cm, flat, upward facing, pale to deep pink, petals usually notched. Needs frequent re-planting as roots tend to become exposed. Sun.

G. goldmanii Mexico ‡40cm Jun—Aug. Mid-green, ruffled leaves; small light mauve-pink flowers with a white eye.

G. gracile **'Blush'**

G. gracile NE Turkey, Caucasus ‡45—70cm late May—Aug. Resembles *G. nodosum* but taller and hairier. Leaves light green and wrinkled. Flowers funnel shaped mid-pink, with short veins, 2.5cm. **'Blanche'** is very pale pink and **'Blush'**, the most common form, mauve pink.

G. grandiflorum see *G. himalayense*

G. gymnocaulon NE Turkey, SW Caucasus ‡30—45cm Jul—Aug. Flowers 4cm, rich violet-blue with darker veins and notched petals. Tends to be short-lived.

G. 'Harmony' (*G. pratense* × *G. collinum*) (Bremner) ‡60—100cm May—Sep. Flowers 4cm, pale lilac-pink veined.

G. harveyi S Africa ‡10cm Grows in mountains at 1300—2000m in rocky ground, forming a cascade of deeply cut and toothed silvery leaves, 3cm, on woody stems. 2cm light pink flowers. Sun.

G. hayatanum B&SWJ 164 Asia: Taiwan, Korea in mountains at 4300m. Collected by Bleddyn Wynn-Jones in Taiwan. A neat mound of velvety, light green, marbled foliage, darkening with age and assuming deep brownish-black blotches. Small, 3cm puce-pink white-eyed flowers with darker veins are carried on sturdy, red trailing stems.

G. himalayense Himalayas ‡30—45cm June, then spasmodically until autumn. Spreading roots give excellent ground cover; finely cut leaves take on brilliant autumn tints. Flowers 5cm, saucer shaped, violet blue flushed reddish pink. **'Baby Blue'** is more compact with 6cm deep-

G. himalayense 'Baby Blue'

G. himalayense 'Derrick Cook'

blue flowers. **'Derrick Cook'** was collected by Derrick in 1984. It is white with purple veins while **'Devil's Blue'** is pale violet-blue. In **'Gravetye'** (syn. *alpinum*) the reddish central zone is more pronounced. **'Irish Blue'** was introduced from Eire by Graham Stuart Thomas; pale blue flowers almost continuously from June to October. **'Pale Irish Blue'** was a seedling from **'Irish Blue'** raised by Michael Wickenden, Cally Gardens. **'Plenum'** (syn. 'Birch Double') has small rounded leaves; flowers 2.5cm, soft lilac blue, flushed with pink, fully double, ↕25cm, not very vigorous. **'Spiti Valley'** is bright blue.

G. ibericum subsp. Ibericum NE Turkey, Caucasus ↕45cm June. Divided leaves with divisions overlapping; numerous lobes and teeth. Flowers 5cm deep violet with darker, feathered veins and notched petals; 'gappy'. Flowering period short but often produces a few blooms in autumn.

G. himalayense 'Devils Blue'

G. himalayense 'Gravetye'

G. i. **subsp.'White Zigana'**

G. i. **subsp.** *jubatum*

G. i. **subsp.** *jubatum* has similar leaves but bluer flowers. **'White Zigana'**, collected by Michael Baron in the Zigana Pass, Turkey, has white, purple-veined blooms 4cm. **'Ushguli Grijs'** (Kramer) has greyish-blue flowers with distinctive dark purple veins; good autumn colour.

G. **incanum var.** *multifidum* S Africa ‡20cm Jun—Aug. This is the form of *G. incanum* commonly cultivated in Britain. Low tussocks of finely cut feathery leaves, dark green above, silvery beneath. Flowers 2.5cm, deep reddish-purple with darker veins, white at centre. Not reliably hardy but can be propagated from seed or stem cuttings. *G. i.* **var.** *incanum* is white.

G. 'Ivan' ^{RHS}♈ (*G. psilostemon?* × *G.* × *oxonianum?*) (Louette) ↕60cm Jun—Sep. Big clumps of handsome leaves resembling those of *G. psilostemon*. The flowers are also similar but more rounded with slightly overlapping petals and concentrated in a great mass just above the foliage.

G. 'Ivan' close-up below and plant habit top right

G. 'Jean Armour' (*G.* × *oxonianum* × *G. traversii*) ↕30cm Jun—Sep. Light pink 2.5cm flowers over grey-green foliage. Sun. Similar to 'Mavis Simpson'.

G. 'Johnson's Blue' (*G. pratense* × *G. himalayense*) ↕30—45cm June onwards. Spreading clumps of finely cut foliage, providing dense ground cover – a strong grower. Flowers 5cm, good lavender-blue, tinged pink at centre, held well above the foliage.

G. 'Jolly Bee' see ROZANNE

G. 'Joy' (*G. traversii* var. *elegans* × *G. lambertii*) (Bremner) ‡30cm Jun—Sep. Named after Joy Jones. A substantial mound of evergreen marbled leaves. The cup-shaped flowers, produced on trailing stems, are pale pink with a silky sheen and reddish-purple veins. Well-drained soil in sun.

G. 'Kanahitobanawa' (*G.* × *oxonianum* f. *thurstonianum* × *G. psilostemon*?) (Sarah and Julian Sutton, Desirable Plants) ‡50cm Jun—Oct. Habit intermediate between parents; forms a big dome; 3cm, starry flowers, vivid magenta-purple with darker veins.

G. 'Karen Wouters' (G. 'Chantilly' × ?) ‡35—60cm, May—Jun. 'Gappy' lavender-pink 3cm flowers; felted foliage. Well-drained soil in sun.

G. 'Kashmir Blue' (*G. pratense* f. *albiflorum* × *G. clarkei* 'Kashmir White') (Louette) ‡60cm Jun-Aug. Similar to *G. pratense* in size and habit with soft, violet-blue flowers.

Karen Wouters

G. 'Kashmir Green'

G. 'Kashmir Green' (*G. clarkei* × *G. pratense*?) (Jansen) ‡40—50cm June onwards. 4cm white saucer-shaped flowers with green veins merging to a small green centre. The leaves are finely cut.

G. 'Kate' (syn. G. 'Kate Folkard') (*G. endressii* × *G. sessiliflorum*) ‡10—15cm June onwards. Named by Oliver Folkard after his daughter. A dwarf plant with small, rounded, cut leaves of bronzy green similar to those of *G. sessiliflorum* 'Nigricans'; sepals also tinged with brown. Flowers 1.5cm, funnel shaped, pale pink with dark veins on thin trailing stems. Needs good drainage and winter protection; tends to die out.

G. 'Khan' (*G. sanguineum* × *G. wlassovianum*?) ‡40cm Jun—Aug. From Wisley Gardens; resembles *G. sanguineum*, though much larger in leaf, flower and height. 5cm flowers produced, in abundance, are a bright magenta-purple.

G. 'Kirsty' (*G. clarkei* 'Kashmir White' × *G. regelii*) (Bremner) ‡50cm May—Jun and later. More compact than 'Kashmir White'. Cut foliage, large cupped white flowers with purple veins.

G. kishtvariense Kashmir ‡30cm Jun—Aug. Introduced by Roy Lancaster (1978). A bushy plant, creeping by underground stolons. Leaves deeply divided with few broad lobes, bright green and wrinkled. Flowers 4cm, facing upwards on thin stems, rich pinkish-purple, white at centre and finely veined.

G. kishtvariense

G. koraiense S. Korea, ‡25cm Jun—Jul. Marbled leaves; lilac-pink, 3cm flowers with dark veins and white eye.

G. koraiense

G. koreanum Korea ‡45cm Jun—Jul. Occurs in wooded mountain areas near streams. Marbled, deeply toothed leaves on trailing stems, colouring well in autumn. 4cm flowers, with separated petals, are rose-pink with deeper veins, pale at the centre.

G. krameri N China, CIS, Korea, Japan, up to 80cm, usually falling into a mound, Jul—Sep. Distinctive leaves, very deeply cut with narrow, coarsely serrated lobes. Flowers 3cm, flat, rose pink with darker veins on long trailing, thin, rather lax, stems. Prefers shade.

G. 'Lakwijk Star' (syn. 'Lyona') (*G. wlassovianum* × ?) ‡35cm Jul—Oct. A widely spreading mound of dark green leaves with deep magenta flowers, 4cm, petals separated.

G. lambertii (syn. *G. grevilleanum*) Himalayas ‡30—45cm Jul—Aug. Trailing plant with few basal leaves. Striking flowers 3cm, nodding, saucer shaped, delicate pale-pink with crimson veining converging into central crimson stain; sometimes reluctant to flower. Best scrambling through other plants or shrubs in partial shade. **'Swansdown'** is the wild white-flowered form: the flowers flushed pink with crimson centres and very pale veins. Leaves mottled with two shades of green. Comes true from seed.

G. libani Lebanon, W Syria, C & S Turkey ‡40cm Apr—May. Flowers 4cm, violet-blue, notched petals and feathery veins. Dormant after flowering until autumn; dark green leaves all winter. For some gardeners, the thick roots tend to lie on the surface of the soil and benefit from mulching, especially in drought conditions.

G. 'Light Dilys'

G. 'Lilac Ice'^{PBR}

G. 'Light Dilys' (van Noort) ↕40cm Jul—Oct. A sport from 'Dilys' with lighter pink flowers and a dark pink eye.

G. 'Lilac Ice'^{PBR} ↕35—45cm Jun—Oct. A sport from ROZANNE, similar to the parent but with pale lilac-pink flowers and light green leaves.

G. × *lindavicum* (*G. argenteum* × *G. cinereum*) up to ↕30cm Jun—Aug. A garden hybrid with deeply cut leaves and strong purple-pink 3cm flowers. Well-drained gritty soil; protect from winter wet. **'Alanah'** is described by the late Walter Ingwersen (1946) as "a very attractive plant, but slightly less silvery in foliage than *G. argenteum* and extremely free in the production of its vivid crimson-purple flowers. It is shy to increase". **'Apple Blossom'** (syn. 'Jenny Bloom') (Bloom) ↕15cm. Flowers palest pink, deeper pink veins. **'Gypsy'** is brilliant pink-cerise with dark veins but is not very hardy. **'Lissadell'** has deep plum-coloured flowers.

G. 'Little David' (*G. psilostemon* × *G. sanguineum* 'Droplet') (Bremner) ↕20—25cm Jun—Sep. Magenta flowers similar to *G. sanguineum* on an erect plant. Difficult to overwinter.

G. 'Little Gem' (*G. × oxonianum* × *G. traversii*) (Bremner) ↕15—20cm Jun—Sep. Similar to 'Russell Prichard' but darker and more compact in habit, making neat mounds of flattish leaves. Not fully hardy, it needs very well-drained soil in full sun and, in cold wet conditions, winter protection.

G. *macrorrhizum* S Europe ↕30cm May—Jun. Reliable ground cover for sun or shade, spreading by underground rhizomes, with copious foliage. A strong grower but not too rampant. Leaves rounded, sticky and aromatic; old leaves colour well in autumn and then die; young leaves remain evergreen. Flowers 2.5cm, dull magenta, reddish bladder-like calyx. Named varieties fall into three colour groups. **'Album'**, **'Lohfelden'**, **'Snow Sprite'**, and **'White-Ness'**^{RHS}♥ are white; most have pink calyces but 'White-Ness' has green. **'Chamce'** and **'Ingwersen's Variety'** are pale pink; **'Bevan's Variety'**, **'Bulgaria'**, **'Czakor'** (Simon), **'De Bilt'**, **'Freundorf'**, **'Mytikas'**, **'Pindus'** (a dwarf plant), **'Prionia'** (smooth leaved), **'Purpurrot'**, **'Ridsko'**, **'Rotblut'**, **'Variegata'** and **'Velebit'** (Simon) are shades of magenta. 'Variegata' is not evergreen, unsuitable for dry shade and less hardy than other varieties.

G. m. 'Album'

G. m. 'Lohfelden'

G. m. 'Spessart'

G. m. 'White-Ness'

G. m. 'Cham-ce'

G. m. 'Ingwersen's Variety'

G. m. Bulgaria'

G. m. 'Pindus'

G. macrostylum S Europe, C & W Turkey 22cm May-June. Leaves small and finely cut, dying down after flowering until autumn. Flowers 2.5cm, rather frail, mauvish-pink with darker veins and centre. There are also lavender-blue forms, net-veined but not dark at the centre. Grows from small tubers which are easily spread when gardening and can be a nuisance; needs well-drained soil in sun so can be container grown. **'Leonidas'** is pink with dark veins but no dark centre, March-May, 30cm.

G. macrostylum 'Leonidas'

G. maculatum NE America ‡40—60cm May—Jul. Erect plant with deeply divided, shiny leaves. Flowers in clusters, 3cm, shallow bowl-shaped, usually pale lilac-pink but can be darker. Petals notched, white at base. Prefers moist soil. **G. m. f. *albiflorum*** is white and **'Beth Chatto'** clear pink. **'Elizabeth Ann'**ᴾᴮᴿ ⏦ has dark reddish-brown leaves and pale purple-pink flowers. **'Espresso'** has lilac-pink flowers and bronze-brown foliage, not as dark as 'Elizabeth Ann'. In **'Spring Purple'** the young foliage is purple; the flowers are deep red-lilac. **'Vickie Lynn'** has purple-pink flowers and leaves which turn orange in autumn.

***G.* 'Madelon'** (*G. psilostemon* × *G. × oxonianum*?) ‡80cm Jun—Aug. 1—2cm flowers, bright carmine with black veins and eye.

G. maderense ⏦ Madeira ‡1m Feb onwards. An architectural giant, growing from an impressive rosette of very large,

G. maderense

G. 'Beth Chatto'

much-divided leaves on brownish-red stems. Flowers 4cm, massed well above the foliage, purplish pink with pale-netted veins, dark crimson centre and dark red anthers. Needs winter protection. May behave as a biennial, dying after flowering, but sometimes grows on from side shoots. Initial growth is rapid and young plants need frequent potting-on so as not to check their progress. Propagated by seed (after storing for a month or two). There is a white-flowered form called **'Guernsey White'**.

G. × magnificum ℞ (*G. ibericum* × *G. platypetalum*) ‡50cm June. A vigorous hybrid, superior to both parents. Leaves nearer to *G. platypetalum*, colouring well in autumn. Flowers 5cm, saucer shaped, rich violet, darkly veined and produced in abundance for a few weeks. Excellent ground cover under shrubs in sun or half shade. This cross has occurred several

times and cultivars have been named but they are generally similar and confused in cultivation. **'Ernst Pagels'** is thought to be a seedling of 'Peter Yeo' but the petals do not overlap. **'Peter Yeo'** has broader bluer petals and **'Rosemoor'** (Simon) is more compact, erect and longer flowering.

G. malviflorum S Spain, Morocco, Algeria ‡20—30cm Mar—Apr. Tuberous rooted with finely cut leaves which appear in late winter; summer dormant. 4cm purple flowers. Needs sun and good drainage; can withstand summer drought.

G. 'Mary Mottram' (*G. endressii* × *G. sylvaticum* 'Album') ‡30cm Jun—Sep. 3cm white flowers fade pale pink.

G. 'Mavis Simpson' ℞ A chance seedling at Kew described in 1982. Makes wide mats of 20cm-high grey-green leaves covered with endless, silvery shell-pink flowers on thin trailing stems all summer into autumn.

G. 'Melinda'[PBR] (*G. endressii* × *G. sylvaticum* 'Mayflower') ‡40—70cm Jun—Sep. Light-pink 2.5cm flowers with red-purple veins; similar to *G. sylvaticum* 'Angulatum'.

G. 'Midnight Star' (*G. × oxonianum* × *G. psilostemon*) ‡60cm Jun—Aug. Leaves

G. 'Midnight Star'

blotched chocolate-brown; flowers purple pink, narrow petalled, 1.5cm.

G. × monacense (*G. phaeum* × *G. reflexum*) ‡50cm May—Jul. Good ground cover with characteristics midway between parents. Leaves usually blotched brown. Reflexed 2cm flowers, dull mauvish-purple with central white and violet zone. **G. m. var. anglicum** (from *G. phaeum* var. *lividum*)

G. 'Mrs. Judith Bradshaw'

G. 'Natalie'

G. m. var. *anglicum*

(see above) has unspotted foliage and lilac-pink flowers. **'Claudine Dupont'** has lime-green spring foliage and grey-purple flowers, April—May; ‡40cm. **G. m. var. monacense 'Breckland Fever'** (Fuller) is rosy-mauve, Apr—Jul, and **'Muldoon'** is maroon pink; both ‡60cm.

G. 'Mrs. Jean Moss' (Moss) ‡60cm Jun—Jul. A seedling from *G.* 'Tidmarsh'. Dark leaves and pink-purple flowers.

G. 'Mrs. Judith Bradshaw' (*G. gracile* × *G. renardii* 'Whiteknights') (Bremner) ‡60—75cm Jun—Jul. Veined pink flowers and lime-green foliage.

G. 'Natalie' (*G. clarkei* 'Kashmir White' × *G. saxatile*) (Bremner) ‡40cm Jun—Aug. 3cm powder-blue flowers.

G. nervosum NW America ‡30—45cm May onwards. A variable plant similar to *G. viscosissimum*, with the same sticky, hairy, characteristics, though the light-green basal leaves are smaller. A single-branched stem of 2—4cm flowers, flat, pale pink to reddish purple with notched petals and dark veins. Will grow in dry shade under trees or shrubs.

G. 'Nicola' (*G.* × *oxonianum* × *G. psilostemon*) (Bremner) ‡60cm, Jun—Aug. 4cm red-purple flowers with widely spaced petals giving a starry effect, (see below).

G. 'Nicola'

G. 'Nimbus' $\overset{\text{RHS}}{\mathbb{Y}}$ (*G. clarkei* 'Kashmir Purple' × *G. collinum*) ‡60—90cm May—Jul. Lax stems and finely cut feathery foliage, often golden tinted when young. Many violet-blue flowers, 3.5cm, held well above the leaves; the petals are red veined and separated.

G. nodosum **'Silverwood'**

G. 'Nimbus' flower and foliage

G. nodosum **'Swish Purple'**

G. nodosum **'Svelte Lilac'**

G. nodosum C Europe ‡30—60cm Jun— Oct. Smooth, shiny foliage; colours well in autumn. Flowers funnel shaped, 2cm lilac pink, with notched petals. Self-sows and will colonise dry soil under trees. **'Blueberry Ice'** (Spiller) is deep velvety-violet with a pale lilac edge (but changes with temperature). **'Clos de Coudray'** is purple with a white edge and **'Hexham Big Eye'** (Moss) similar to 'Svelte Lilac' but larger. **'Julie's Velvet'** (Julie Ritchie, Hoo House Nursery) is a red-purple seedling from **'Whiteleaf'**. **'Silverwood'** (Joan Taylor) has light green foliage and white flowers ‡20—30cm. **'Svelte Lilac'** is lilac with dark veins and **'Swish Purple'** dark-veined violet-purple, pale at the centre; the foliage is darker than usual. **'Whiteleaf'** (Lionel Bacon) has deep purple flowers with a white edge; the name comes from the raiser's house.

G. 'Nora Bremner' (*G. rubifolium* × *G. wallichianum* 'Buxton's Variety') (Bremner) ‡25cm Jun—Sep. Mounds of marbled foliage with the same rambling habit as *G.* 'Buxton's Variety'. The flowers are 4cm, soft violet-blue with a large white centre and finely veined, separated petals. Unfortunately it is not easy to propagate.

G. 'Nunwood Purple' (*G. pratense* f. *albiflorum* × *G. himalayense* 'Gravetye') ‡30cm Jun—Jul; repeats. Blue-purple flowers with overlapping petals, 4.5cm.

G. 'Old Rose' (*G.* × *oxonianum* 'A T Johnson' × *G. versicolor*) ‡40cm Jun—Oct. Light green foliage; 2.5cm flowers deep pink fading to pale pink.

G. oreganum W. USA ‡60cm Jun—Jul. Leaves similar to *G. pratense*, making substantial clumps. Prolific flowers 5cm, saucer shaped and deep rose-purple.

G. orientalitibeticum SW China ‡20cm Jun—Jul. Discovered by E H Wilson. Leaves marbled with lime green. Flowers 2.5cm purple-pink with a white centre. Tuberous rooted and tends to be invasive.

G. 'Orion' ℞ ‡70cm Jun—Jul. Floriferous seedling from 'Brookside'. 6cm deep violet-blue flowers with red veins and a white eye.

G. orientalitibeticum

G. 'Orkney Blue' (*G. ibericum* subsp. *jubatum* × *G. gymnocaulon*) (Bremner) ‡40cm Jun—Jul. Leaves and 4cm heavily veined blue flowers intermediate between parents.

G. 'Bremerry'[PBR] ORKNEY CHERRY (*G. antipodeum* × *G.* × *oxonianum*) (Bremner) ‡25cm Jun—Oct. Brown leaves; flowers bright cherry-pink with a white eye, 2.5cm. Sun and good drainage.

G. 'Orkney Pink' (*G. antipodeum* × *G.* × *oxonianum*) (Bremner) ‡15cm Jun—Oct. Chocolate-purple foliage and 3cm dark pink flowers on spreading stems. Sun and good drainage.

G. **'Orion' plant and close-up**

G. × oxonianum (*G. endressii* × *G. versicolor*) ‡30—50cm. Most flowers are funnel shaped and many are 3cm diameter; their main flush is Jun—Jul but flowering continues to October. This fertile cross, which will hybridise with other species, has given rise to a great variety of cultivars. **'A T Johnson'** ♀ᴿᴴˢ is light rose-pink, introduced before 1937. **'Ankum's White'** is white and **'Beholder's Eye'** ♀ᴿᴴˢ purple-pink with a white eye. **'Breckland Sunset'** (Fuller) has red-purple flowers, strongly veined, while **'Bregover Pearl'** is pale pink, faintly veined. **'Bressingham's Delight'** (Bloom) is dark salmon-pink, strongly veined; **'Chocolate Strawberry'** (Moss) has heavily brown-blotched foliage and strawberry-pink flowers; **'Claridge Druce'** ‡60cm is a vigorous plant with large 4.5cm purple-pink flowers with darker veins (1900). In **'Coronet'** the 2cm reddish-pink flowers have petaloid stamens which look like extra petals, giving a crown-like centre. **'Elworthy Misty'** (Spiller) is a seedling from 'Walter's Gift' with similar foliage but deep pink flowers. **'Frank Lawley'** (Moss) is pale pink with separated petals. **'Fran's Star'** (Crûg) is a cross between 'Southcombe Double' and 'Walter's Gift'; it has foliage similar to the latter and 2cm pink semi-double flowers. **'Hexham Pink'** (Moss) is a compact plant with deep pink 4cm bowl-shaped flowers with overlapping petals; **'Hexham White'** (Moss) is white with a green eye. **'Hollywood'** (Langthorn's, Essex) has showy 4cm flowers with magenta veins over a pale pink background; **'Julie Brennan'** (Judith Bradshaw, Catforth Gardens) is light purple with dark-red veins. **'Kate Moss'** (Moss) is very pale pink, 2cm. **'Katherine Adele'** was a seedling from 'Walter's Gift' at Heronswood; it has darker brown markings

G. × o. 'Ankum's White'

G. × o. 'Elworthy Misty'

G. × o. 'Frank Lawley'

G. × o. 'Pat Smallacombe'

G. × o. 'Rebecca Moss'

G. × o. 'Rosenlicht'

G. × o. 'Sandy'

G. × o. 'Phantom'

than the parent over a larger part of the leaf. The 2.5cm flowers have purple veins over a very pale background. **'Kingston'** has strong crimson veining over a pale background and **'Lace Time'** a pale background with purple veins (2.5cm); the young foliage of the latter is yellow green. Grown by Margery Fish at East Lambrook Manor, **'Lady Moore'** has 4cm veined mid-pink flowers. '**Lambrook Gillian**' is light pink and not strongly veined; there is some confusion over this plant in cultivation. **'Laura Skelton'** has 4cm white flowers, heavily veined in purple. **'Maurice Moka'** has brown-blotched leaves and pale-pink flowers; **'Miriam Rundle'** is dark pink and **'Music from Big Pink'** (Moss) mid-pink, darkening with age. **'Pat Smallacombe'** has 4cm purplish-pink flowers with a white eye and is very heavily veined. **'Pearl Boland'** is white, ageing pink, and **'Phantom'** (Tuite) bright pink with darker veins, the leaves heavily brown-spotted. **'Phoebe Noble'** from Vancouver Island is one of the darkest cultivars, having intense magenta-pink, heavily veined flowers.

G. × o. f. *thurstonianum*

G. × o. f. *thurstonianum* variability

G. × o. f. t. 'David McClintock'

G. × o. f. t. 'Sherwood'

G. × o. f. t. 'Southcombe Double'

G. × o. 'Wargrave Pink'

'Phoebe's Blush' (Moss) is pale pink and darkens with age. **'Prestbury Blush'** is white with pale veins; the light green leaves have small brown blotches. **'Rebecca Moss'** (Moss) is pale pink and **'Rose Clair'**, which was raised in 1940 by A T Johnson, rose salmon. **'Rosenlicht'** has purple-pink flowers and **'Rosemary'** light pink but both fade. **'Sandy'** is pale pink. **'Spring Fling'** is notable for its yellow-variegated young foliage; pink flowers. **'Stillingfleet Keira'** has bright pink flowers with light veining and **'Summer Surprise'** is bright pink with a white eye, 4.5cm. **'Susie White'** (Moss) is very pale pink. **G. × o. f. *thurstonianum*** has 4cm flowers with very narrow, widely separated, petals, reddish-purple, white at the base; the foliage is sometimes blotched. **'Armitagea'** is red purple with a white centre, 2.5cm. **'Breckland Brownie'** (Fuller) has heavily marked brown leaves and violet flowers with white edges. **'David McClintock'** is similar to the type but has flowers that are richer pink with darker veins. **'Red Sputnik'** is deep reddish-pink, **'Robin's Ginger Nut'** (Moss) salmon pink and **'Sherwood'** (Bremner) pale pink, veined purple and twisted. **'Southcombe Double'** has 2cm semi-double, deep pink flowers and some single; **'Southcombe Star'** has a more sprawling habit and is deep mauve-pink; both are sterile. **'White Stripes'** is white with light

G. palmatum

pink veining and wider petals. **'Trevor's White'** (Trevor Bath) is white, changing to pale pink with age or heat; it was originally known as *G. endressii* 'Album'. **'Wageningen'** ^{RHS} is salmon pink. **'Walter's Gift'**, when introduced in 1989, was distinctive for the chocolate-brown zones spreading from the centre of the new leaves and has been used in breeding; the flowers are pale pink with red-purple veins. **'Wargrave Pink'** (‡60cm) is salmon pink with overlapping petals, **'Waystrode'** very pale pink, veined, **'Westacre White'** (Tuite) white, veined light purple, and **'Winscombe'** very pale silvery-pink, darkening to deep pink.

G. palmatum ^{RHS}   Madeira ‡35—90cm Jun—Jul. Resembles *G. reuteri* but with hardly any rosette stem and greener stalks. Rosettes very large, leaves can be 30cm or more across. Flowers 3cm, prolific, mauve pink, crimson centre. May need winter protection in colder areas; makes a showy pot plant. Propagated from seed.

G. palustre E & C Europe ‡30—45cm Jun—Aug. A low-growing, bushy plant with light green leaves. Flowers 3cm, trumpet shaped, bright magenta-pink with dark veins, white at the centre. Self-sows freely.

***G.* 'Brempat'** Patricia ^{RHS}   (*G. endressii* ×

G. Patricia

G. psilostemon) (Bremner) ‡90cm Jun—Sep. Resembles *G. psilostemon* although the 4cm flowers are a softer colour; large leaves, 23cm in width. Full sun.

G. peloponnesiacum Greece ‡45—60cm May—Jun. Slate-blue 4cm flowers in clusters on long stems. Summer dormant.

G. 'Perfect Storm (*G. traversii, G. sessiliflorum* and two other species) (Bremner) ‡30cm Jun—Sep. Prostrate soft, grey-green foliage. Magenta-pink flowers with heavy veining and a black centre.

G. phaeum Mountains of S & C Europe ‡60cm May—Jul. The 'Mourning Widow' geranium is so called because of its unusually dark flowers. Leaves divided and sometimes blotched with purplish brown in the notches. Flowers 2.5cm, flat, very dark maroon, white at centre. Petals often slightly frilled round the edge. Excellent for quite dry shady areas, where it will colonise and hybridise if other forms are grown. **'Advendo'** is reddish lilac, **'Album'** white, **'Alec's Pink'** mauve pink (early flowering) and **'All Saints'** (Monksilver) pale lavender-pink. **'Angelina'** has dark red flowers with reflexed petals and a large dark brown zone on the leaves. **'Blauwvoet'** is blue with a white centre, **'Blue Shadow'** (Fuller) amethyst blue, **'Calligrapher'** dull purple with a pale grey eye and **'Chocolate Chip'** (Robin Parer) dark brown-maroon. **'Conny Broe'** has spring foliage, netted yellow, and wine red flowers. **'David Martin'** is dusky pink with a white eye and **'George Stone'** wine red. **'Golden Samobor'** has yellow spring foliage changing to heavy dark brown blotching, maroon flowers. **'Golden Spring'** has pale golden leaves

Typical phaeum habit ('Lady in Mourning' above)

and dark red-purple flowers; **'Green Ghost'** (Moss) is white with yellow-green leaves. **G. p. var. hungaricum** has very dark, almost black, reflexed petals and a mauve-grey eye. In **'James Haunch'** the leaves have creamy-yellow and brown markings; plum-purple flowers. **'Judith's Blue'** (Moss) is dusky blue, **'Klepper'**

G. phaeum

G. p. 'Album'

G. p. 'Angelina'

G. p. 'Judith's Blue'

G. p. var. *lividum* 'Majus'

G. p. 'Raven'

G. p. 'Ray of Light'

G. p. 'Blue Shadow'

G. p. var. *hungaricum*

G. p. 'Marchant's Ghost'

G. p. 'Mierhausen'

G. p. 'Rose Madder'

G. p. 'Shadowlight'

G. phaeum - close -up of flower

purple with a white centre, **'Lady in Mourning'** black violet with a white eye, to ⭡90cm, large flower, **'Lavender Pinwheel'** pale lavender with violet veins and a dark picotee rim and **'Lilacina'** deep lilac-blue ⭡90cm. **'Lily Lovell'** (Bath) is deep violet. **'Lisa'** has pale green leaves with a central yellow mark and dark red flowers. *G. p.* var. *lividum* is very pale mauve; the form **'Joan Baker'**, a seedling raised by Bill Baker, is light mauve with a dark ring around the centre. **'Majus'** has large lilac flowers with a blue ring around a white centre. **'Lustige Witwe'** has irregular creamy-white markings on the foliage and deep brown-maroon flowers. **'Marchant's Ghost'** is pale grey-lavender and **'Margaret Wilson'** is blue purple with pale reticulation on the foliage; **'Mierhausen'** is similar to the species but with paler, rounder flowers. **'Mojito'**, a seedling from 'Margaret Wilson', has yellow-striped foliage and grey flowers. **'Mrs. Charles Perrin'** is mauve pink with a paler eye, **'Night Time'** dark slate-purple flowers and darkly blotched leaves; **'Nightshade'** has unspotted leaves and dark purple flowers. **'Our Pat'** ⭡ is tall, ⭡1m, with yellow-green leaves and dark-purple flowers with a white eye. *G. p.* var. *phaeum* **'Langthorn's Blue'** is dull blue-purple with a white centre. **'Samobor'** is dusky purple; the leaves are strongly blotched purple-brown in a ring around the centre. **'Phantom of the Opera'** (Moss) is purple pink with a light eye; some leaves are cream variegated. **'Rachel's Rhapsody'** (Rachel Etheridge) has yellow-variegated leaves and purple flowers;

'Raven', a seedling from 'Lily Lovell', has purple-blotched leaves, maroon flowers. **'Ray of Light'** (Fuller) is white, changing to blush, with dark leaf markings. **'Rise Top Lilac'** (Bath) is pale lilac, **'Rose Air'** pale pink and **'Rose Madder'** (Bath) brownish pink with a grey eye. **'Sericourt'** (Bob Brown) has deep red-brown flowers and bright yellow spring foliage; it should be grown in shade because the leaves burn in strong sun. **'Shadowlight'** has leaves with central yellow markings and dark chocolate spots; maroon-purple flowers. The spring foliage of **'Springtime'**[PBR] is green, red and white; dark purple flowers. **'Stillingfleet Ghost'** has large lavender-grey flowers, **'Taff's Jester'** maroon, with spring foliage marked cream, maroon and grey. **'Variegatum'**, maroon, has leaves splashed irregularly with cream and touches of bright, reddish pink, while **'Walkure'** has light blue flowers with a central blue ring and light green leaves.

G. 'Philippe Vapelle' (*G. renardii* × *G. platypetalum*) (Louette) ‡38cm Jun—Jul. Soft, hairy deciduous leaves with a velvety texture, similar to but larger than those of *G. renardii*. Widely separated petals, bluish purple and strongly veined (3.5cm).

G. 'Philippe Vapelle'

G. 'Pink Delight' (*G. antipodeum*? × *G.* × *oxonianum*?) ‡10—20cm Jun—Sep. A seedling found by Juliet Robinson. Soft, grey-green leaves; shell-pink flowers with purple veins. Sterile. Needs well-drained soil and sun.

G. 'Pink Penny' (syn. 'Jolly Pink') (*G. wallichianum* 'Syabru' × *G.* ROZANNE) (van Noort) ‡30cm Jun—Sep. Marbled foliage spreading to 1m; flowers 3.5cm, bright magenta-pink with dark purple veins. Best in some shade.

G. 'Pink Penny'

G. platyanthum (syn. *G. eriostemon*) NE Asia, E Tibet, W China, Korea and Japan ‡45—60cm May—Jun. A hairy plant with large, wrinkled leaves, colouring well in the autumn. Flowers 3cm, nearly flat, in dense clusters on erect stems; slatey-mauvish pink with small white centre. **G. p. var. reinii** is a compact form.

G. p. var. reinii

G. 'Turco'

G. platypetalum Caucasus ↕30—45cm Jun—Jul. Similar to *G. ibericum* but leaves not so deeply cut and less sharply toothed; soft and grey-green. Flowers 4cm, deep violet-blue with strong dark veins. Well-drained soil in sun. **'Turco'** has larger flowers with a white eye and a pale patch in the middle of each petal. 'Genyell' appears to be the same plant and since 'Turco' was collected first (in Turkey) this is probably a synonym.

G. pogonanthum SW China, W & N Burma ↕45—60cm Jul—Sep. Clumps of light green, marbled leaves. Flowers 3cm, dusky pink with narrow, reflexed petals. Takes a year or two to establish and then needs regular replanting if the roots work their way to the surface.

G. pratense N Europe, Asia ↕60—90cm Jun—Jul. The 'Meadow Cranesbill' has divided leaves, and tall, branching stems with 4cm saucer-shaped flowers in shades including deep blue, pale blue, pink and white with varying degrees of veining. Seeds prolifically. Double forms have smaller flowers (2.5cm) and do not seed. **'Blue Lagoon'** is light royal-blue, **'Cluden Sapphire'** purple-blue with pale veins and **'Else Lacey'** double or semi-double very pale blue with a pink centre. **'Hocus Pocus'** has lavender-purple flowers and bronze-tinged foliage. **'Mrs. Kendall Clark'** ^{RHS}⚘ is violet blue with white veins, said to come true from seed.

G. p. 'Mrs. Kendall Clark' above & below

G. p. 'Cluden Sapphire'

'**Plenum Caeruleum**' is violet blue with petals pinkish at the base and '**Plenum Violaceum**' ℞ is violet, flushed pink; both

G. p. '**Plenum Violaceum**'

G. p. var. *pratense* f. *albiflorum* '**Laura**'ᴾᴮᴿ

are old cultivars and fully double. '**Wisley Blue**' is pale-violet with light veining (red). *G. p.* var. *pratense* f. *albiflorum* ↕40cm is white and all white-flowered plants come into this classification. '**Algera Double**' has semi-double white flowers with a purple centre. '**Bittersweet**' (Monksilver) has very pale lavender-pink flowers with pale veins; the young leaves are tinged with purple. '**Double Jewel**' is double white with a purple centre; '**Galactic**' (syn. 'Album') is white and vigorous but mildew-prone. '**Laura**'ᴾᴮᴿ is a white double, as is '**Plenum Album**' ↕50cm, an old cultivar, needing good soil and frequent division. '**Rose Queen**' has white flowers veined red. '**Silver Queen**' (A T Johnson, 1926) is very pale lilac-blue. '**Striatum**' is white

G. p. var. *pratense* f. *albiflorum* '**Striatum**'

G. p '**Wisley Blue**'

G. p. subsp. *stewartianum* '**Elizabeth Yeo**'

streaked with violet and **'Pink Splash'** is a pink form of 'Striatum'. **'Yorkshire Queen'** ↕1.2m has white flowers veined purple. ***G. p.* subsp. *stewartianum* 'Elizabeth Yeo'** ↕0.7—1.5m high, usually less than 1m, has 5cm dark pink flowers May—Jun and later. Collected by Dr. Raina in Kashmir, it was named by Dr Peter Yeo after his wife. The **'Victor Reiter'** seed strain, developed in California in the 1970s, results in variable leaf colours from plain green, through bronzy green, to very dark purple. A selection from it has been micro-propagated as **'Victor Reiter Junior'**. **'Midnight Reiter'** is a seed strain developed from Victor Reiter: beetroot-coloured leaves and 2cm 'gappy' deep-blue flowers. **'Nodbeauty'**[PBR] BLACK BEAUTY (*G. pratense* Victor Reiter × *G. pratense* 'Mrs. Kendall Clark') ↕40cm, has dark green, almost black, foliage, darkest in spring; violet flowers in flushes until autumn. **'Midnight Blues'** has violet-blue flowers and purple-black leaves; it is darker and more vigorous than most of the Victor Reiter Group. **'New Dimension'**, ↕30cm, has 'gappy' lavender-blue flowers and dark purple-green leaves and **'Purple Heron'** very dark black-burgundy foliage and violet flowers ↕45cm.

G. 'Prelude' (*G. albiflorum* × *G. sylvaticum*) (Bremner) ↕45—90cm May and later. Pale mauve 2.5cm flowers.

G. 'Prelude'

G. procurrens

G. procurrens Himalayas ↕30cm July onwards. Rampant ground cover for dry areas, sending out long prostrate stems which root at the nodes. Flowers 2.5cm, subdued purple with a black centre, into late autumn.

G. psilostemon ♆[RHS] (syn. *G. armenum*) NE Turkey, SW Caucasus ↕90—120cm Jun—Aug. A stunning border plant with large, deeply cut leaves, turning red in autumn. Flowers 4cm, bowl shaped, intense magenta-crimson, accentuated by a black central zone and dark veins. Best in sun but will tolerate some shade. **'Bressingham Flair'** (Bloom) is a paler form, **'Coton Goliath'** taller and **'Jason Bloom'** (Bloom) earlier with larger flowers (5—6cm).

G. psilostemon **'Jason Bloom'**

G. pulchrum S Africa ‡90cm Jul—Aug. Sub-shrub: stems woody and quite thick at the base. Leaves soft, velvety, silvery grey-green, undersides covered with silvery silky hairs, almost white; handsomely fingered and sharply serrated. Flowers 3cm, mauvish pink, sometimes white at centre. Less hardy than most.

G. pylzowianum W China ‡15—25cm May—Jun. Leaves rounded, finely dissected; flowers 2cm, deep clear pink. Travels rapidly by chains of small tubers; suitable for containers, paving or the edge of a path in sun.

G. pyrenaicum SW & W Europe ‡30—50cm May—Oct. Mounds of nicely rounded, evergreen leaves. Flowers 1.5cm, mauvish pink with notched petals freely produced on thin stems. Rather too weedy for anything but the wild garden;

G. p. 'Isparta'

self-sows abundantly. More desirable are **G. p. f. albiflorum**, with 2cm starry white flowers which show up particularly well in shade, and **'Bill Wallis'**, rich purple-violet 2cm flowers and less vigorous. **'Isparta'**, collected in the Isparta Province of Turkey by Peter Yeo, ‡50—60cm, has 2.5cm pale violet-blue white-eyed flowers continuously from early summer into autumn.

G. p. 'Isparta'

G. p. f. albiflorum

G. 'Red Admiral'

G. renardii foliage and flower

G. 'Red Admiral' (*G. psilostemon* × *G. sylvaticum* 'Baker's Pink') (Foster) ↕45—60cm Jun—Sep. Deep red-pink with black veins and centre, 4cm.

G. reflexum S Europe ↕45—60cm May—Jun. Similar to G. *phaeum*; leaves usually blotched dark purplish-brown where divisions meet; nodding flowers 2cm rosy mauve, strongly reflexed, narrow petals, white at base. Likes shade.

G. refractum Himalayas, N Burma, SW China ↕45—60cm Jun—Jul. Deeply divided, sometimes marbled leaves. Flowers nodding, 2.5—3cm, white or pink, narrow reflexed petals, red stamens. Distinguished by purple hairs on the upper parts. Probably best in sun.

G. regelii Himalayas ↕30—55cm May—Jun. 4cm pale blue flowers resembling a compact version of G. *pratense*.

G. renardii ^{RHS}♚ Caucasus ↕30cm June. Sage-green leaves, soft, velvety to the touch, with a distinctive scalloped shape. Flowers 4cm, white (very slightly blue) with purple veins; petals widely spaced. Said to do best

in poor soil in sun. **'Rothbury Hills'** is more vigorous than the type, with larger flowers; **'Tschelda'** (Simon) is also 5cm, pale blue-purple. **'Whiteknights'** is a clone selected from seedlings raised at Reading University using seed collected in the wild; more robust than the type and not so compact with 4cm violet-blue flowers. **'Zetterlund'** is pale mauve.

G. reuteri (syn. *G. canariense*) Canary Islands ↕60cm May onwards. Basal rosette of deeply divided large aromatic leaves, growing from a stem a few inches above the soil; leaf stalks flushed brownish purple. Numerous flowers, 4cm, deep pink, rather widely spaced petals, pale on the underside, often white at the base. Not fully hardy and short-lived (up to three years). Greenhouse or warm sheltered position in well-drained soil in milder areas. Propagated by seed.

G. richardsonii W N America ‡30—60cm May onwards. Deeply divided, shiny, green leaves with pointed lobes. Flowers 3cm flat, white or tinged with pink, lightly veined. Likes plenty of moisture.

G. richardsonii

G. × riversleaianum (*G. endressii* × *G. traversii*) **'Russell Prichard'** ☑ pre-1915 ‡20—40cm mounds of small, silvery-grey-green foliage. Flowers 3cm bright magenta-pink on trailing stems, prolifically produced from July onwards. Not reliably hardy.

G. rivulare W & C European Alps ‡45cm May—Jun. 2cm white, funnel-shaped flowers with violet veins; deeply divided leaves.

G. robustum S Africa ‡60—100cm Jun—Sep. A fairly hardy sub-shrub, stems woody at the base; ferny grey-green leaves silvery on the underside. Flowers 3cm, mauvish pink or pale purple, shallowly notched petals. Sun; withstands drought well. Self-sows occasionally.

G. 'Rosie Crûg' (*G.* × *antipodeum* × *G. lambertii*) ‡20cm Jun—Aug. The open, slightly nodding, flowers are very pale and finely veined with rose pink from a stronger pink central zone; low mats of pewter-bronze foliage. Full sun; needs sharp drainage.

G. ROZANNE^{PBR}

G. 'Gerwat'^{PBR} ROZANNE ☑ (*G. wallichianum* 'Buxton's Variety' × *G. himalyense*) ‡50cm Jul—Oct. A seedling found in the garden of Donald and Rozanne Waterer and introduced by Blooms of Bressingham. The plant proved difficult to propagate, taking several years before being launched at Chelsea 2000. It is vigorous with wide-spreading stems up to 120cm, having foliage of the *G. wallichianum* type, which colours well with age. The 4cm flowers are deep violet-blue with a white centre and prominent black anthers.

G. ROZANNE^{PBR}

G. ruprechtii Russia ‡60cm Jun—Jul. Dark-violet 4.5cm flowers.

G. 'Russell Prichard' see G. × *riversleaianum*

G. 'Bremigo'^{PBR} Sabani Blue (*G. ibericum* subsp. *jubatum* × *G. libani*) (Bremner) ‡45cm April onwards. Violet 4cm flowers, 'gappy' when mature. Tends to be dormant late summer and then grow new leaves to overwinter.

G. s. 'Max Frei'

G. Sabani Blue^{PBR}

G. s. 'Vision Violet'

G. 'Salome' (*G. lambertii* × *G. procurrens*) ‡90cm Jul—Sep. Long, trailing, non-rooting, stems emerge from a comparatively small mound of gold-tinged, marbled leaves. The 3cm flowers are pale violet-purple with deeper veins and a black eye.

G. 'Sandrine'^{PBR} (*G.* 'Ann Folkard' × *G.* Patricia) Similar to 'Ann Folkard' but with a larger (5cm) flower.

G. s. Alan Bloom^{PBR}

G. sanguineum Europe, Caucasus, N Turkey ‡22—30cm Jun—Jul and later. The 'Bloody Cranesbill' found on western coasts of Britain including the Gower. Forms wide mats of tangled stems with small rounded leaves, finely cut, turning brilliant shades in autumn. Flowers 3cm, saucer shaped,

G. s. 'Catforth Carnival'

G. s. 'Elke'

G. s. var. *striatum*

G. s. 'Apfelblute'

G. s. 'Album'

purple magenta. Grows naturally on sand dunes and in limestone but is successful in borders. Named forms, some wild-collected, are mostly in shades of magenta and flower size is often 4cm: **'Alpenglow'**, **'Barnsley'**, **'Bloody Graham'** (Graham Stuart Thomas), **'Canon Miles'** (2.5cm), **'Cedric Morris'** ‡40cm, **'Elsbeth'** (Simon), **'Feu d'Automne'**, **'Inverness'** (Jack Drake), 'Joanna', **'John Elsley'**, **'Little Bead'** ♆, , **'Max Frei'**, **'New Hampshire Purple'** (syn. 'Purple Flame' ‡40cm) **'Nyewood'**, **'Rod Leeds'** ‡40cm and **'Vision Violet'** ‡40cm. Strong pink occurs in **'Bloger'**PBR ALAN BLOOM (Bloom), **'Ankum's Pride'** (Jansen), **'Belle of Herterton'** (Moss), **'Holden'**, **'Shepherd's Warning'** (Drake) and **'Vision Light Pink'**. 'Aviemore' ♆ (Drake), **'Catforth Carnival'** (Bradshaw) and **'Glenluce'** are deep mauve-pink; **'Elke'** has a pale edge to the petals. *G. s.* var. *striatum* ♆ (syn. *G. lancastriense*), from Walney Island in Lancashire (now Cumbria), is very pale pink with pink veins, as is the form **'Splendens'** ♆ and **'Apfelblute'**, a selection from it. **'Album'** ♆ is the only white form.

G. **'Sanne'** (*G. sessiliflorum* × *G.* × *oxonianum*) ‡25cm May—Sep. Forms a carpet of small brown leaves and 1.5cm white flowers, (non-stop).

G. 'Sanne'

G. 'Scapa Flow'

G. 'Scapa Flow' (*G. renardii* × *G. ibericum* subsp. *jubatum*) (Bremner) ‡35cm Jun—Jul. Leaves similar to *G. renardii*; flowers flat, 4cm, soft blue with violet veins.

G. schlechteri S Africa ‡50cm Jun—Aug. Wide-spreading bushy plant with a woody base and silvery evergreen divided foliage. 2.5cm funnel-shaped pink flowers. Well-drained soil in sun.

G. sessiliflorum subsp. **novae-zelandiae** **'Nigricans'** New Zealand ‡7cm June onwards. Neat rosettes of small, rounded, brown leaves and 1cm white flowers. Needs good drainage. Self-sows moderately. **'Porters Pass'** has red-brown foliage.

G. shikokianum S Japan, Korea ‡20—40cm July onwards. Compact clumps of deeply cut, light green leaves, often with yellowish-green marbling. Good autumn colour. Flowers on longish stems, funnel shaped, 2.5cm pink with white centre, netted with purple veins. Dislikes hot dry conditions, best in shade, scrambling through low shrubs. **G. s. var. quelpaertense** is lower growing and hairier.

G. shikokianum var. yoshianum

G. sinense SW China ‡60cm Jul—Aug. Shiny olive-green leaves, deeply divided and faintly marbled. Flowers 2cm, similar in shape to *G. phaeum*, very dark (almost black) velvety reflexed petals, coral at the base, black anthers and crimson stigma. Plants slow to establish, building up to a substantial mound. Shade and moist soil.

G. `Sirak' $\overset{\text{RHS}}{\text{♀}}$ (*G. gracile* × *G. ibericum*) (Simon) ‡35—50cm Jul—Oct. Plants of this cross raised independently by Alan Bremner and Hans Simon are identical and so were given the same name. 5cm flowers, bright pinkish-purple with darker veins.

G. `Sirak'

G. soboliferum CIS, Manchuria, mountains of C & S Japan ‡30—40cm Jul—Sep. Small clumps of finely cut feathery leaves. Flowers 4cm, saucer shaped, reddish purple with dark veins. Needs plenty of moisture in full sun. **Cally** strain, with rich colouring, was selected from Russian seed. **'Starman'** is lighter pink with crimson markings, 4.5cm.

G. soboliferum
Cally strain

G. 'Solitaire' (*G. libani* × *G. peloponnesiacum*) (Bremner) ‡40cm Apr—Jun. 3cm violet flowers, winter-green.

G. 'Spinners' (*G. pratense* × ?) ‡0cm Jun—Jul. Deep purple-blue, 3cm, bowl-shaped flowers and finely cut foliage.

G. 'Spinners'

G. 'Stephanie' (*G. peloponnesiacum* × *G.renardii*) ‡30—40cm Apr—May. Foliage and flower shape typical of *G. renardii*; pale violet, veined purple.

G. 'Storm Chaser' (*G. traversii* × *G. procurrens* × *G. lambertii*) (Bremner) ‡30cm Jun—Aug. Lilac pink with a dark eye, 3cm.

G. subcaulescens ♀ Balkan Peninsula, C & NE Turkey ‡22cm May—Jul. Low-growing mounds of dark green leaves. Fierce magenta flowers 2.5cm, very dark centre and dark veins, black anthers. Needs good drainage. **'Giuseppii'** ♀ has more silvery leaves, near-magenta flowers with less-pronounced central area. **'Splendens'** ♀ is less strident in colour with a dark centre.

G. 'Sue Crûg' (*G.* × *oxonianum* × *G.* 'Salome') ‡40cm Jun—Sep. Flowers similar to 'Salome' but 4cm; purplish-pink separated

G. 'Sue Crûg'

petals, strongly veined with near-white streaks down the centres. The dark central eye is less prominent. Mid-green, slightly marbled, foliage resembles that of the other parent, *G.* × *oxonianum*, and is on trailing stems from a basal mound.

G. 'Summer Cloud' (*G. collinum* × *G. clarkei* 'Kashmir White') ‡45—70cm Jul—Sep. Sprawling habit; flower similar to 'Kashmir White' but smaller (3cm).

G. 'Gernic'PBR SUMMER SKIES (*G. pratense* × *G. himalayense* 'Plenum'?) ‡60cm Jun—Jul. Shorter than the double forms of *G. pratense* and coming into bloom earlier. Fully double flowers are lavender blue with overtones of pink and a green centre. Full sun and fertile soil.

G. SUMMER SKIESPBR

G. swatense Swat division of Pakistan ↕30cm Jun—Sep. A low-growing, sprawling plant from a thick taproot; mottled leaves on long, thin, reddish stems. Flat 4cm flowers, purplish pink with purple anthers but variable. Not easy to please and liable to die out.

G. 'Sweet Heidy' [PBR] (*G. wallichianum* × ?) ↕35cm May—Oct. 'Gappy' 4cm blue-purple flowers with a white centre surrounded by a pink ring; prostrate habit.

G. sylvaticum Europe, N Turkey ↕60—75cm May—Jun and later. The 'Wood Cranesbill' is found wild in areas such as Weardale. An upright plant with broadly fingered, light green leaves, attractively lobed and toothed. Flowers 2.5cm, saucer shaped, purplish violet with white centres, in profusion. ***G. s. f. albiflorum*** is the wild white form with some pink colouring in sepals, stamens and stigmas. **'Album'** [RHS ♛] has no pink pigment; it seems to come true from seed. **'Amy Doncaster'** is deep blue with a white eye, 3cm; **'Angulatum'** ↕90cm has 4cm light pink flowers with pink veins on angled stems. **'Birch Lilac'** is similar to the species but lilac, while **'Coquetdale Lilac'** (Moss) has 4cm lilac flowers with light veining. **'Greek Fire'**

G. sylvaticum 'Mayflower'

(Moss), grown from wild-collected seed, is described as red. **'Ice Blue'** (Jansen) ↕45cm is bluish lilac and **'Mayflower'** [RHS ♛] (Bloom) pale violet-blue, white-centred, both 3.5cm. ***G. s. f. roseum* 'Baker's Pink'**, a natural pink variant collected by A W A 'Bill' Baker, has 3cm clear shell-pink blooms over a long flowering period. **'Silva'** is pale violet and ***G. s.* subsp. *sylvaticum* var. *wanneri*** plummy pink with rose-red veins.

G. 'Tanya Rendall' [PBR] (*G. antipodeum* 'Black Ice' × *G.* × *oxonianum*) ↕15cm May—Sep. Bright pink-purple, 2.5cm flowers with a white eye over olive-brown foliage, which spreads to 60cm. Sun.

G. 'Terre Franche' (*G.* 'Philippe Vapelle' × *G. platypetalum*) (Louette) ↕45—60cm Jun—Sep. Petals separated, violet blue with purple veins; 4cm.

G. thunbergii N China, Taiwan, Japan ↕22cm Jul—Oct. A vigorous, sprawling plant; semi-evergreen leaves, light green with dark blotches where divisions meet. Flowers 1.5cm varying from white to purplish pink. Rather

G. sylvaticum 'Album'

G. thunbergii white form

weedy but useful ground cover for dry shade. **'Jester's Jacket'** has red-backed golden leaves in spring which become red-and-white variegated; pink flowers. It comes true from seed.

G. 'Tinpenny Mauve' (Elaine Horton) ‡60cm Jun—Sep. A chance seedling at Tinpenny Cottage. 3cm mauve-blue flowers with rounded, overlapping petals.

G. 'Tiny Monster' (syn. ROLF ROYCE) (*G. sanguineum* 'Ankum's Pride' × *G. psilostemon*) ‡50cm Jul—Sep. A vigorous plant with 4cm flowers, crimson red-purple with dark red veins.

G. transbaicalicum Siberia‡25cm Jun—Jul. Similar to (or a subspecies of?) *G. pratense*; the leaves are edged brown and the flowers a deeper shade than usual.

G. traversii var. elegans Chatham Islands ‡15—20cm Jun—Sep. Compact rosettes of silver-green cut leaves. Flowers 2.5cm, saucer shaped, milky pink and finely veined, on leafy stems which tend to flop and lie on the surface of the soil. Well-drained gritty soil in full sun. Not completely hardy, needing some protection in winter. Self-sown seedlings occasionally appear.

G. tuberosum Mediterranean ‡20—40cm late Apr—May. Grows from moderately spreading tubers, with ferny leaves in spring; summer dormant. Flowers 2.5cm, pale pink with deeper pink veins, on erect stems. Requires good drainage and sun.

G. versicolor (syn. *G. striatum*) Europe ‡45cm May—Jun. A bushy plant, similar to *G. endressii*, forming hummocks of light green, blotched leaves that remain fresh in winter. Dainty flowers, trumpet shaped, 2.5cm, white with a network of fine magenta veins. Good ground cover for sun or shade. Hybridizes freely with *G. endressii*. **'Snow White'** (syn. 'White Lady') is an all-white form.

G. viscosissimum W N America ‡30—60cm June and often later. An attractive, sticky plant, with large, hairy, divided leaves and sharply toothed segments, similar to *G. nervosum*. Flowers 3cm, in clusters, bright rose-pink to purple, on strong, branching, stems. Sun.

G. versicolor

G. versicolor 'Snow White'

G. wallichianum 'Buxton's Variety'

G. wallichianum Himalayas ‡30cm Jul—Oct. Long trailing stems with shallowly divided and marbled leaves. A variable species, the flowers come in shades of blue, mauve and pink, 3cm, saucer shaped, usually with white centres. **'Buxton's Variety'** is violet blue, bluer when cold. It is the best-known form (syn. 'Buxton's Blue) and was discovered c.1920 in the garden of E C Buxton in Betwys-y-Coed. It has a deep taproot so division is difficult and propagation is usually from seed, selecting plants with the best blue flowers. **'Crystal Lake'**[PBR] (from *G. w.* 'Silver Blue') (Kramer) has a more upright habit ‡50cm and light violet-blue flowers with purple veins. **'Noorthava'** Havana Blues is light blue, **'Rainbow'** blue purple at the edges merging to reddish purple and **'Rise and Shine'**[PBR] (van Noort) cobalt blue with a pink tinge on ageing; all have dark veins. **'Rosetta'** (from 'Syabru') is pink with a light-pink centre, while **'Shocking Blue'** is typical of the species. **'Syabru'**, collected in Nepal, is magenta and **'Sylvia's Surprise'**[PBR] pink.

G. wallichianum 'Crystal Lake'[PBR]

G. wlassovianum

pink with dark centre. Reasonably hardy in a sheltered position, naturalising where happy. Sometimes affected by virus that distorts the petals (in which case the plants should be destroyed).

G. wlassovianum E Siberia, Mongolia, Far East, CIS, N China ‡30—45cm Jul—Aug. A clump-former with attractive foliage emerging pinkish bronze in spring. Mature leaves are dusky green tinged with brown, velvety in texture, assuming brilliant red autumn colour, darkening to purplish brown before dying away. Flowers 3cm, deep purple-violet with darker veins and a white eye. **'Blue Star'** is dark bluish-purple.

G. yeoi (syn. *G. rubescens*) (biennial) Madeira ‡60—90cm May onwards. Resembles a large Herb Robert. Flower and leaf stalks beetroot-red from impressive rosette. Flowers 2.5cm numerous, bright

G. yesoense C & N Japan, Kuril Islands ‡30—45cm Jun—Aug. A bushy plant similar to *G. dahuricum*; leaves very deeply and sharply cut. Flowers 3cm saucer shaped, pink with darker veins, or white. Not a particularly garden-worthy plant but suitable for light woodland or a wild garden in moisture-retentive soil.

G. yunnanense SW China, N Burma ‡45—60cm Jun—Jul. Leaves deeply divided, yellowish green and marbled; flowering stems lax. Flowers 3cm, nodding, bowl shaped, deep pink with dark anthers. Sun; not easy to grow.

G. wlassovianum foliage autumn colour

Further Information

The following have Plant Heritage National Plant Collections®:

Geranium sylvaticum
Gary Bartlett, Riddle Road Allotments, Riddle Road, Sittingbourne, Kent ME10 1LF.
bartlett4@supanet.com
07720 892 704
Open by appointment.

Geranium sylvaticum and *renardii*
Susan Clarke, Wren's Nest, Wrenbury Heath Road, Wrenbury, Nantwich, Cheshire CW5 8EQ.
01270 780 704 wrenburysue@gmail.com
Best time to view is May-Jul. Open by appointment.

Geranium phaeum **Group**
Jean Purkiss, 1 Kelton Croft, Kirkland, Frizington, Cumbria CA26 3YE
01946 862 664 expressplants@aol.com
Best time to view is May–Jun.

Geranium × *cantabrigiense, macrorrhizum* and *sanguineum*
Margaret Stone, Brockamin, Old Hills, Callow End, Worcestershire WR2 4TQ
01905 830 370 stone.brockamin@btinternet.com
Phone or check HPS or Plant Heritage website for open days.
Best time to view is late May for *macrorrhizum* and × *cantabrigiense;* June to early July for *sanguineum.*

Geranium nodosum
Joan Taylor, Silverwood House, Gardeners Lane, Romsey, Hantshire SO51 6AD
0238 081 4345 joanvtaylor@hotmail.com www.birchwoodplants.co.uk
Best time to view is June. Open by appointment.

Geranium **spp. & primary hybrids**
Mrs S Petitt, Cambridge University Botanic Garden, 1 Brookside, Cambridge CB2 1JE
01223 336 265 enquiries@botanic.cam.ac.uk www.botanic.cam.ac.uk

The following nurseries selling geraniums have display gardens:

The Plantsman's Preference, Church Road, South Lopham, Diss, Norfolk IP22 2LW
01379 710 810/07799 855 559 www.plantpref.co.uk

Elworthy Cottage Plants, Elworthy, Taunton, Somerset TA4 3PX
01984 656 427 www.elworthy-cottage.co.uk

Avondale Nursery, at Russells Nursery, Mill Hill, Baginton, near Coventry, CV8 3AG
024 7667 3662/0797 9090 3096 www.avondalenursery.co.uk

Societies

The Hardy Plant Society, Hardy Geranium Group www.hardy-plant.org.uk/geranium

Photographic credits

The HPS has been granted publishing rights for these photographs–copyright remains with the photographer.

Hardy Plant Society would like to thank the following for permission to reproduce their photographs. Many of these photographers are contributors to the Hardy Plant Society's Digital Image Library www.hardy-plant.org.uk/imagelibrary

Key: page number followed by position on page, ie top left to bottom left, then top right to bottom right

Adrian James: 29-2, 29-3, 50-3,
Alan Whitehead: 53-3
Ann Hooper: 19-3, 34-1,
Blooms of Bressingham®: 18-2, 49-2, 49-3
Carrie Thomas: 29-4, 33-4, 38-1, 47-1, 57-3
David Victor: 6-3,
Don Witton: 48-3
Eleanor Fisher: 20-3, 32-5,
Ilja Smit-Kroon: 43-2, 43-3
Irene Tibbenham: 39-2
Jennifer Harmer: 6-1, 10-1
John McCormack: front cover, 39-1, 42-1, 44-4, 47-2, 47-3
Ken Mines, Picket Lane Nursery: 37-1, 37-5
Margaret Stone: 14-2, 54-2, 56-2
Ruth Jowett: 30-2
Tim Fuller, The Plantsman's Preference: 9-1, 10-2, 10-4, 10-5, 13-1, 14-1, 15-2, 16-1, 16-2, 16-3, 17-1, 17-3, 17-5, 18-1, 18-3, 18-4, 20-1, 20-2, 21-1, 23-2, 24-1, 24-2, 26-1, 27-1, 28-1, 28-2, 29-6, 30-1, 31-2, 32-1, 32-3, 32-4, 33-1, 33-5, 34-3, 35-1, 35-2, 35-3, 35-4, 36-1, 36-2, 36-3, 36-4, 36-5, 37-1, 37-2, 37-3, 37-4, 37-5, 40-2, 40-3, 40-4, 40-5, 40-6, 41-1, 41-2, 41-3, 41-4, 41-5, 41-6, 44-1, 44-2, 44-3, 45-1, 45-2, 46-1, 46-2, 46-3, 48-1, 49-1, 50-1, 50-2, 50-5, 51-3, 51-5, 52-1, 52-3, 52-4, 55-1, 55-3
Trevor Hards: 45-3
Trevor Walton: 29-5, 48-2, 50-4
Tricia Fraser: 6-2, 8, 9-2, 9-3, 9-4, 10-3, 15-1, 17-2, 19-1, 19-2, 21-2, 22-1, 23-1, 23-3, 23-4, 25-1, 25-2, 26-2, 27-2, 29-1, 31-1, 33-2, 33-3, 34-2, 38-2, 40-1, 43-1, 45-4, 45-5, 51-1, 51-2, 51-4, 52-2, 53-1, 53-2, 54-1, 55-2, 56-1, 57-1, 57-2